The Key of Forgiveness

Unlocking the door for a more powerful Christian walk

Glenn H. Smith Jr.

THE KEY OF FORGIVENESS-

The KEY of Forgiveness

Unlocking the door for a more powerful christian walk

Glenn Smith Jr

Forward by Calvin B. Harris Ph.D

The Key Of Forgiveness-

THE KEY OF FORGIVENESS-

ewpublishing.com

Published by

Eagle's Wings Publishing

Central Point, OR 97502

2008 ©Eagle's Wings Publishing

ISBN -10:   0-9849362-1-0
ISBN -13:   978-0-9849362-1-5

All scripture quotations, unless otherwise indicated, are taken from the New King James Version®. Copyright © 1982 by Thomas Nelson, Inc. Used by permission. All rights reserved.

Acknowledgments

Any time you set out on a creative adventure, you want to have people around you who can help you navigate through the various obstacles that stand in the way of completion. In my case, this was never more important than on this project.

This was my first attempt at writing a book. I would now like to bring to attention and thank the people who helped me find the finish line intact.

First, I must recognize that none of this would, or could, happen without God in my life. I have done my best to both follow the lead of the Holy Spirit and the directive of God in the writing of this book. It is both to God and through God that I can do all things. That being said, thank you Jesus!

I also want to say thanks to my beautiful wife, Mary, and my great children for putting up with me for all of these years. I know I can be at bit stubborn, so thanks for the support you have shown, I love you all.

There are many others who have been vital to the success of this project. Pastor Steve and the leaders at Joy Christian Fellowship, your guidance and wisdom has been more than valuable in my life.

Dr. Calvin Harris, I thank you for being both a solid counselor as well as a beloved family member. Your kind words have encouraged me greatly. Pete and Amy Miller, your editing was superb. I look forward to many more times of "working" over my "stuff". Thank you for keeping me away from the abyss. Roger Fredinburg, thanks for keeping me on my toes.

I want to also thank all of my close friends for being there when I became frustrated or discouraged. Without you all, I might never have gotten this far.

Finally, to Ray Beeson. Your information has been greatly appreciated.

Glenn Smith Jr.

THE KEY OF FORGIVENESS-

Contents

Acknowledgments vi

Forward 3

Introduction 5

Preface 7

What is Forgiveness? 9

My Story 17

Forgiveness Saves a Nation 27

Jesus' Teaching on Forgiveness 39

Binding and Loosing 53

The Most Powerful Spiritual Weapon 59

Stephen and Paul 65

The Goats 73

Forgive Yourself 79

Accessing God's Forgiveness 85

THE KEY OF FORGIVENESS-

Forward

My belief is that each of us that has been given the gift of a successful life (or not so successful) has an obligation to share our experiences and strengths gained as we live our lives fully and share the path that led us to our own personal truths. The reader will find this text is instructive and inspiring; it offers the reader the benefit of the hills and pot holes of the author's road well-traveled as well as the opportunity to learn from his many challenges and victories.

As a senior university professor for nearly twenty-five years, I am often asked to read and edit text books but seldom have the opportunity to read literature that has been written by a person that I have known since the day of his birth and have had the honor of watching him turn into a fine musician, businessman and now scholar.

Glenn's book will leave you with no doubt that he has benefited from discovering and nurturing a personal and strong relationship with God and how his focus for living is to follow Jesus Christ's example and teachings as close as any human can do.

This book has great utility for those that struggle with the day-in-and-day-out challenges that face each of us as we interact with others. When God's Will is the cornerstone, all is well; when the individual's will is the template for interacting with others it is suggested that there will be problems on the horizon. Glenn explains in detail how we can spot many of the negative consequences of self-will and prescribes the exact solution.

The reader might keep a Holy Bible close at hand while reading this fine book as you may be inspired to look up the various references that inspired Glenn Smith and that he shares with you.

This book, like an eternal building stands on the concrete truths found in both the ancient scripture and the more modern New Testament.

Calvin B. Harris Ph.D.
Sr. Professor, Park University
Founder MSA Inc

Introduction

Glenn Smith has taken on a daunting task of writing a book on a doctrinal theme like forgiveness. The challenge is to make it interesting, informative, personal, and spiritually uplifting. Well, He did it!

"The Key of Forgiveness" is a very fast moving read on the various areas of the Biblical theme of forgiveness. Glenn is transparent and vulnerable as he shares his personal encounters with the challenge of and the result of receiving and giving forgiveness. It is not merely a compilation of scriptures on the subject matter, but is a weaving of scriptural proofs woven with practical application and wisdom.

Reading this volume brings one back again to the conviction of the absolute necessity of practicing forgiveness as well as receiving God's forgiveness.

Matthew 18:21-23 '..."Lord, how often shall my brother sin against me, and I forgive him? Up to seven times?" Jesus said to him, "I do not say to you, up to seven times, but up to seventy times seven."'

Pastor Steve Schmelzer
Joy Christian Fellowship
Medford, Oregon

THE KEY OF FORGIVENESS-

Preface

Have you ever had one of those moments when the whole direction of your life changes? In the fall of 2005, that very thing happened to me. I was driving to work when I sensed God challenging me to write down all of the different messages that I had received or taught throughout my years as a Christian. When I arrived at my office and had my coffee, I commenced with this strange project. What I ended up with was a list of over 30 different subjects, quite varied in content. Sitting there, looking it over, I pondered why God would have me do this. It was not as if I was looking for something new to do. At the time, I was well established in my automotive career and fairly content with how things were going. Then came the moment when I realized the purpose of the list. I was being called upon to study and prepare to write about these subjects.

The list included the concept of forgiveness as a powerful spiritual tool — a literal key to unlock the door to a full and powerful Christian walk. This would become the subject that I would write about first, thereby launching me into a whole new chapter in my life. Pun intended. So that you know, I'm a fairly accomplished musician, but I never did see myself becoming a writer. The truth is that I am not a prolific reader, nor am I some great master of the English language, I'm just a drummer. Still, wanting to be obedient and follow what I perceived was God's directive, the journey began. So here it is — a book on forgiveness.

Starting out, my thought was to write about the theological views on this subject, and to some degree, I have. But as I proceeded through the writing process itself, I found myself involved in a great deal of self examination regarding my own walk of forgiveness. What began as a simple teaching quickly became quite personal in nature. As you read what I believe God has had me write, I want to encourage you also to be self-examining. I truly believe that forgiveness is possibly the most crucial act we can exhibit as Christians. It is not just some cool concept, but a critical life choice. To be like Jesus, we must live like Jesus. In order to live a truly full and vibrant life, as I have discovered, forgiveness is a must. My hope and prayer is that, as you read on, God will touch you in the same way that he has touched me. I hope to show you the true value of living a life that includes total forgiveness.

Chapter 1

What is Forgiveness?

"Forgiveness ought to be like a canceled note – torn in two and burned up so that it never can be shown against one." — Henry Ward Beecher (1813-1887), U.S. Congregational Minister

Have you ever heard someone say, "I will forgive you, but I will never forget what you did"? Is that forgiveness? How about this one: "If you apologize first, then I will forgive you"? Or "I can forgive you for this, but not for that." We all do this, thinking that somehow we are in the right. I suppose, if we look at it from a superficial point of view, we might be. But is that how God views it? Is this how God wants us to live? Well then, "What is true forgiveness anyway?"

To fully understand the concept of forgiveness, we must first define it. Webster's dictionary states that to forgive is to grant relief from payment of a debt. In other words, when you forgive a debtor, they no longer owe anything to you, and they are free from that bond. According to this definition whatever you were bound by, be it a contract or a promise, when it is forgiven, is no longer in force.

Here is an example of something that my wife and I did many years ago. We had sold a mobile home to a very nice young couple on contract. They had a couple of children and were just getting started in life. About three years into the contract, they fell upon hard times and were struggling to make the payments. After talking to them and praying about it, we decided to waive all of the remaining balance and signed over the title to them. We fully released them from any further obligation for that contract. This would be an example of forgiveness.

Again from Webster, another definition of forgiveness is to give up resentment (or the claim for requital) of an insult, and to cease to feel resentment against the offender. In this example, you give up your claim to the offense. This is something that is not done easily. The problem with resentment is that it usually harms the offended more than the offender. Here's a quote from an unknown author that I really feel puts this in proper perspective: "Resentment is like a glass of poison that a man drinks. He then sits down and waits for his enemy to die."

In many ancient pagan societies, forgiveness was considered to be a weakness rather than a virtue, since retaliation was the social norm. Forgiveness often came with strings attached. To just let something go for no apparent reason was typically not culturally acceptable.

Today, unfortunately, this happens far too often. As a result, a rights-based society has developed in which the primary goal is to look out for self. As time goes on, many people begin to lose their ability to feel compassion. Instead they lean toward being cold and heartless, while believing that they are somehow projecting strength. Sadly, this does not come as a complete surprise since the American culture is becoming more and more pagan all the time. While there seems to be little trouble in accepting the concept of God's existence, problems arise as people are challenged to believe in one God Almighty. In turn, by rejecting the concept of the Almighty God being supreme, people find it far easier to discount God's ways of doing things. One result of this viewpoint is a selfish and manipulative version of forgiveness; the one that doesn't truly release things, but rather chooses to retain the obligation for later use. So, again, what is true forgiveness?

I believe that true forgiving must include forgetting. If we genuinely forgive someone and release them, we should also forget. Now, you may ask, what if I was really hurt or ripped off by someone? Do I just pretend it never happened? These are good questions. If we want to please God, then the answer is "Yes." We must move beyond the things that hurt us by learning to forget. No, it is not easy, but neither is it impossible.

Remember the mobile home deal. When I sent the title and said that there was no further payment due, that was it; it was over. At that point I had to call it good and forget the rest of the contract. Only then could I say, "It is forgiven." If I didn't do this, I would have left open the option to come back and try to collect later.

Of course, it is human nature to remember. The truest test of my forgiveness shows up later, say, during a time of need. If I were to fall on hard times, with a real push to find money fast, I could remember that the contract was never fully paid and call the young couple up to collect. But that would have just been wrong.

The same thing is true if I refuse to let go of a hurt, and continue to hold it out there, even after it was supposedly forgiven. So why then does it seem to be perfectly acceptable to say, "I forgive but won't forget"? It's bad enough that this is common in secular life, but should it be this way in the church, too?

The point here is that if God doesn't work in this manner, then neither should we. The hardest part is letting go. Human nature tends to resist forgetting because it requires giving up a right. However, that is exactly what God does — He forgets. In Jeremiah 31:34, God is speaking of the end of days when He says, *"I will forgive them their iniquity and their sin I will remember no more."* Also, in Psalm 103:12, it says, *"As far as the east is from the west, so far has he removed our transgressions from us."* In Isaiah 38:17 it says, *"...you have cast all my sins behind your back."* This sounds to me like God's brand of forgiveness is to forgive and forget. You just cannot escape this. Isaiah 43:25 repeats the theme; *"I, even I, am He who blots out your transgressions for my own sake, and I will NOT remember your sins."*

Wow! Since God forgets, shouldn't we also? But we don't, do we? Instead, we are often pride driven in our attempts to protect the so-called rights and standing we desire. Our selfish feelings then take precedent over the needs of others. We neither want to be wrong or wronged. Today, the general attitude is that someone else is probably at fault for the things that happen. The driving force behind that attitude is a strong desire for vindication and closure, hoping that it will bring about better feelings. Does this ring a bell? Again, remember the pagan viewpoint, forgiveness is a weakness. I do not believe that God wants us to live as pagans, as the Bible certainly doesn't support that kind of lifestyle. What I do believe is that to truly forgive, we must forget.

The Bible speaks of the need to put away selfish ambitions and subdue the flesh nature. I think our resistance to true forgiveness is directly related to our refusal to die to our selfish desires. Yet forgiveness is a great way to subdue that selfish nature in all of us. When you forgive someone unilaterally, without any prompting or response, you are giving up your right to be angry and bitter. You are literally walking away from the need for self-vindication. Author and minister, E. H. Chapin said, "Never does the human soul appear so strong as when it forgoes revenge and dares to forgive an injury." This certainly doesn't sound like a weakness to me.

God says that vengeance is His, not ours. We are not to look for revenge but instead for peace. When we continue to retain offenses instead of forgetting, we run the risk of growing bitter and unloving. These were not qualities that Jesus possessed. If we are to be true followers of Jesus, we have to work to be like Him. Jesus walked a perfect life. He lived without sin or malice. He did what the Father did, and in the end, He forgave all of us on the cross. This forgiveness was given without our asking.

Let me clarify something here. We must repent of our sins, ask for salvation, and then believe to be saved—this is commanded. I am not contradicting this. Because we bear the guilt of whatever sins we have committed, we must ask God for His forgiveness. By His grace, we are saved when we repent. My point is that after we repent and are saved, we must also learn to walk in the same realm of forgiveness in which Jesus walked. To truly be called Christian, that is, one who is Christ-like, we must do what Christ did and forgive, with or without being asked.

Interestingly, you can travel north only so far before you begin to go south. But if you travel east, you will always be going east until you stop and turn around. East never runs into or becomes west. The same is true with forgiveness. To go eastward, away from an offense, is the only way for us to truly live a life of forgiveness. It turns into unforgiveness only when you turn back. Just remember, forgiveness is not an option — it is commanded.

In the following chapters, we will be looking at how forgiveness can set you free from the bonds of strife and bitterness. We will see how Jesus both taught and lived a life of forgiveness. I will also show some examples of people who did and who did not display an understanding of the principle of living forgiveness. So as you read through the rest of this book, continue to ask yourself, "How I am living?"

THE KEY OF FORGIVENESS-

Chapter 2

My Story

"For someone with no forgiveness in their heart, to live is worse than death."
— *Mr. Miyagi, Karate Kid 2*

One evening after work, I was watching television and heard the above quote. As I sat there pondering those words, it caused me to reflect on my own life.

Generally speaking, I like to think of myself as a fairly decent person. I usually try to get along with others and stay out of trouble. But through the years, I have had to deal with occasional bouts of anger. Periodically, I found myself going through what are usually considered the normal trials of life while thinking that, to me, they seemed seriously unfair. Often, when faced with these kinds of problems, I would look for the best angle that served my own interests. I would spend my time fantasizing or rationalizing the different ways in which I was the one who was in the right. My goal would be to have the best possible light always shining on me. It was not necessarily my style to consider the actual reasons why things turned out the way they did. To live this way was quite easy for me. I could simply ignore my own contributions to the problem and focus on others.

If this sounds familiar, it should. Jesus addressed this subject in Matthew 7:3-5: *"And why do you look at the speck in your brother's eye, but do not consider the plank in your own eye? Or how can you say to your brother, 'Let me remove the speck from your eye,' and look, a plank is in your own eye?"*

Of course, I knew what God wanted me to do. But because of my predominate pride, I proudly did my own thing. Living this way often left me wounded, and caused many battle scars. I would occasionally find myself even growing bitter about hearsay, without the benefit of proof. Eventually I began to have doubts about my ability to be successful, which led to periods of intense depression. Very few people ever really knew what was going on inside of me, since I could be quite the actor at times. If you asked me how I was doing, I would politely say "fine," even if you were the one I had the problem with at the time. I would put on my "happy face," raise the facade, and hide the truth. A better way to put it is that I was a hypocrite. The saddest part about it was being so deeply involved in the church we attended, yet feeling so detached at the same time.

I built up many years of selective forgiveness, picking and choosing who or what I felt was deserving of my forgiveness. Often, if there was some sort of benefit to be gained from holding on to an offense, I would retain it. This created for me a vicious cycle of near-success followed by failure to advance. It was affecting virtually every aspect of my life. I really didn't understand why. I prayed to God for many things (finances, health, ministry opportunities, and more), but it seemed that even God wasn't really listening. I finally came to the point where I actually believed that I was cursed and no longer needed; just a failure waiting to be discarded. It was during this time that God began to reveal to me the genuine power of forgiveness.

Now, I will be the first to admit that I can be a stubborn and prideful man. Because of this, it took God a while to break through, but He did prevail. In 2001, I was experiencing a major downturn in my finances. Having gone through this before, I was worried. Our family was in a position to lose everything, and a miracle was needed. Near the end of May of that year, our church welcomed a guest speaker from Africa, Dr. Charles Mugo. Through the words of Dr. Mugo, God spoke about the real source of my trouble. It was ME, refusing to be completely obedient to His commands regarding the principal of tithing. I had literally become my own worst enemy.

Over the twenty years or so since I had become a Christian, I had sat through many different teachings regarding giving, so I was not ignorant about the subject. Giving was not so much the problem. What I struggled with was the actual tithing principle (the giving of ten percent of my income). I suppose it was really because of fear, but I simply could not bring myself to write that check every month. I knew all of the great arguments as to why I didn't have to. I had rationalized my position, until I was convinced that I was right. And it was all working beautifully, for my demise.

God touched me that Sunday morning. Dr. Mugo spoke about the needs of the people in the mission field who were working to bring the gospel of Jesus to the foreign lands. As he was explaining why the tithe was so important in supporting the local church, he made this statement: "If you want Jesus to be alive in your business, be obedient; fund the work." I was stunned. There I was, arguing with God, telling Him to stay out of my business. I had literally set myself up to fail by my own disobedience. It was after the service, during the ministry time, that it finally sunk in. God would forgive me and wipe the slate clean if I would simply trust Him and believe that all of His words were true from that point on. I had to give up and let go.

Even though I was not a new Christian, I still wrestled with areas of trust. Since I knew what God's word said about faith, the only excuse I had for being in that situation was my own pride. That morning I apologized to God and asked Him to forgive me. I pledged to be obedient and trust Him.

This may not seem to have much to do with the subject of this book, but I can tell you that it has everything to do with it. It was a difficult admission. I knew that my stubbornness was the problem, but I was having a difficult time letting it go. I had a need to be right, and releasing my pride didn't fill that need. In order to change my circumstances, I had to release both my pride and my fear. Only then could God deal with the larger problem, my unwillingness to forgive.

It seemed, at that time, that I had little and sometimes no forgiveness in my heart. It was clouding my ability to see things properly. A series of things had happened in my life that left me bitter inside. Although I would talk about forgiving, I was not fully releasing the things that were hurting me. I wasn't living forgiveness. That day I experienced God's mercy as I was able to begin to let go of the things that had bound me for years. This was the start of God showing me the value of complete forgiveness. That newfound freedom that I felt gave me a renewed vigor to search God's Word. Revelation started flowing. I am also happy to report that our finances recovered and that God was again true to His Word. We didn't lose a thing.

Now I don't want to spoil the mood, but things seldom go untested. Since Satan never just lets things go, I was in for the most intense test of my Christian walk.
Looking back, my wife and I became Christians in 1982. We started attending a church with some friends, but things went a bit sour after a couple of years, so we left. We were searching for a new church when, through a business contact in March of 1984, we showed up at Joy Christian Fellowship. There we met Pastor Steve Schmelzer. My wife, Mary, and I were somewhat hurt and confused, due in part to the way in which we had left the previous church. Pastor Steve, after hearing why we were there, welcomed us in. This was an exciting time. The little church was brand new, with less than twenty people in attendance. It seemed like the perfect place to land. Although we started out as curious onlookers, eventually we became very involved. Within a few months of our arrival, God impressed upon me the need to bind myself to Pastor Steve and not leave his side. God had now placed me with a mentor. For many years I have stood by him while our church was rocked by different upheavals, yet, through it all, God always kept our relationship strong. After many years, my wife and I have developed a solid and fruitful relationship with our pastor, both in the church and as friends. We have even helped raise each other's children, literally.

I say all of this because it was the strength of that very relationship that was to be tested in order for God to really establish in me the absolute power of forgiveness.

Near the end of the summer of 2003, Pastor Steve and my wife and I became involved in a very tense disagreement about something that had happened. I am not going to go into the details because, frankly, they are not important. The point here is that we had a big problem. Things had been said, feelings had been hurt, and everyone had their position. No resolution was in sight. The contention had built to the point that my wife and I were now meeting with Pastor Steve for the purpose of leaving the church.

Remember my pattern to rationalize and create the best light for myself? This, having been born from my pride, was the tool now being used to try to destroy a very special relationship. Through the years, I have seen families leave the church in anger. It is always both painful and destructive when it happens. I was fully aware that leaving in this manner was going to cause problems, especially at home, but onward in anger I marched.

It was during this meeting that God spoke to me. I know that it is a strange thing to say that I heard God speak, but I tell you that I know what I heard was from God. While I was in the middle of defending my position, He spoke in a voice that I will never forget. He said that I could leave, and would be justified in doing so. I had every right and no one could fault me. Wow! Was God really telling me to go? This could have been a great moment for self-justification. But something about what He said didn't feel right. Since I was greatly troubled by this, I asked God what He really wanted me to do. After reminding me how He had placed me with Pastor Steve, God then asked me if I had heard anything from Him that changed that charge. Honestly, I couldn't think of anything. Though I was still very puzzled, I could only come to one conclusion. God wanted me to stay!

This is where the rubber meets the road. Do I serve my own interests or God's? How many times do we all face this kind of test, and fail? The choice I had to make required me to humble myself and give up my justification to leave. I had to believe that God had my best interest in mind, even if I didn't necessarily agree with Him at the time. I had to swallow my pride.

Right then, I stopped the meeting and, much to my wife's surprise, announced to my pastor and great friend, "We are not going anywhere so this will have to be worked out because God wants us right here." It was one of the hardest things I ever had to do. I had to forgive the things that had been said before I was even asked. I had to let go of my right to be angry. God still had a future plan for us in this place, and my pride had almost completely derailed it. I like what Bishop Desmond Tutu once said: "Without forgiveness, there is no future."

Of course, this did not resolve the problem, and much damage had been done. The truth is that the tension actually grew for a while. But after some time, changes began to happen. I had resigned my position in the music department, and my wife had stepped away from her duties in the children's ministry. There was much healing and repairing needing to be done, and we needed the time to allow God to complete it. There were many years of bitterness that had to be worked out. I had to learn to accept the fact that I was as much of the problem as anyone. I also had to learn to forgive myself, as well as others. I discovered that as I forgave, God forgave. This is the law of sowing and reaping. Sow forgiveness and reap forgiveness.

The work had begun, forgiveness had been extended, and after a year or so, things began to return to normal. In time, we resumed many of our functions within the church, including some new responsibilities. By releasing the hurt and anger, God was able to intervene and set things right by His standard, while restoring the relationship with our pastor.

Today, my friendship with Pastor Steve is better than it has ever been. God has opened up exciting new ministry opportunities for my wife and me, including the writing of this book. Our entire family is serving God, and there is a great peace in our lives. Since I have been growing in this life of forgiveness, I no longer try to rationalize things, nor do I take things as personally as before. Instead, I try to give them to God right up front. My life is infinitely better, all as a result of learning the lesson of the power of forgiveness.

It is sad to think that you can go through your whole life trying to be right all of the time and completely miss out on the joy of simply being loved. Bitterness is a trap that leads to depression and eventually self-destruction. But forgiveness leads to salvation. God has proven that time and time again.

I want to close this chapter with wisdom from the book of James. In chapter 3, verses 13-18: *"Who is wise and understanding among you? Let him show by good conduct that his works are done in the meekness of wisdom. But if you have bitter envy and self-seeking in your hearts, do not boast and lie against the truth. This wisdom does not descend from above, but is earthly, sensual, demonic. For where envy and self-seeking exist, confusion and every evil thing are there. But the wisdom that is from above is first pure, then peaceable, gentle, willing to yield, full of mercy and good fruits, without partiality and without hypocrisy. Now the fruit of righteousness is sown in peace by those who make peace."*

Chapter 3

Forgiveness Saves a Nation

"You will know that forgiveness has begun when you recall those who hurt you and feel the power to wish them well."
— *Lewis B. Smedes, Author*

"Forgiveness does not change the past, but it does enlarge the future."
— *Paul Boese, Television Producer*

Life can be cruel. Sometimes things happen that hurt us deeply. Divorces, separations, family cruelty, and misunderstandings all can leave deep psychological scars. Then there are the physical attacks like rape or abuse. All of this is awful and leaves people wounded and upset. While in the midst of all of this, it is very difficult to find yourself defaulting to a position of forgiveness. Forgiving is not a natural reaction to the things that offend or wound. Instead, anger and bitterness develop, as well as an endless search for revenge. At best, the desire is to at least get even. It is human nature to serve self and look out for number one.

I often wonder how God feels about this. In the world this is normal behavior, but in the Kingdom of God it should not be. There will be no unforgiveness or bitterness in heaven, so why have it here?

People betray each other. They do things that offend and disappoint. But as Christians, we have to expect it. Jesus said it would be that way, so we are without excuse. Moving past our base human nature requires a complete trust in God. We must learn to see God as our vindicator. To do this we must be truly willing to forgive. Getting this down is crucial to our well being and might possibly even save our families from destruction. George Herbert, a 16th century poet, wrote, "He who cannot forgive breaks the bridge over which he himself must pass."

In preparing to write this book, studying and praying, I came across several examples of people who learned to live life in a state of forgiveness. Let's take a look at two of them now and see the long-range effects of their actions.

Joseph

Anyone who has been in Sunday school or around Bible teaching has heard the story of Joseph and his multi-colored coat. His life is also an interesting study in living forgiveness.

Genesis chapters 37, and 39-45, records the story of Joseph. He was the first-born child of Rachel, Jacob's most beloved wife. Jacob favored Joseph over all of his other children, thus causing a considerable amount of envy and jealousy to arise among the ten older brothers. Jacob honored Joseph with a coat of many colors, setting him apart from his brothers. How many times do we see this in our society today? One child is preferred over another, leaving someone to feel slighted. It causes a person to become bitter and envious, and even feel unloved. I don't believe Jacob consciously meant any disrespect toward his other sons, or that he necessarily loved them any less. He simply showed preference to the child of his most-loved wife.

As time went on, Joseph had prophetic dreams. These dreams showed him that he would eventually stand over his family in a significant position of authority. Since Joseph was still young, 17 to be exact (Genesis 37:2), he excitedly shared these dreams with his family. As he did, he became even less popular with his brothers, while not exactly pleasing his father either. God was setting up the opportunity to bring future salvation to His chosen people, even though they had no idea they were going to need to be saved. But, because of the anger and jealousy that was now smoldering within his brothers, the decision was made that Joseph had to go.

At first, the brothers talked about just killing him, but that was determined to be too extreme. So they took his coat and threw him into a pit until they could decide what to do. After much discussion and disagreement, it was decided. He would be sold to some Ishmaelite traders who were passing by. Later, the Ishmaelites sold him into slavery in Egypt. At this point it would not be hard to imagine Joseph developing a serious case of bitterness towards his brothers. Even though he had come from a somewhat dysfunctional family, it was still his family. It must have been confusing for Joseph. First he was picked on, abused, and rejected. Then he was sold into slavery and sent to a far away land, never to be seen again. I don't know about you, but by now I would probably be blaming everyone for all of this, maybe even God, but that didn't seem to be the case with Joseph. Yes, I am sure there was plenty of anger and uncertainty, but as you read on about his life, he seemed to know how to move past it. Somewhere along the way, he must have seen God's hand in his life and decided to let go of the anger. One reason I believe this to be true is found in Genesis 39:2. It says, *"The Lord was with Joseph and he was a successful man."* If he had been bitter with God and still walking with unforgiveness towards his family, I am not sure that God would have been so strong with him. God will not coexist with sin, and unforgiveness is a sin.

Of course, Joseph's troubles were far from over. In Egypt, he was sold as a slave into the house of Potiphar, one of Pharaoh's officers. Potiphar entrusted Joseph with his household and there Joseph prospered. That was until Potiphar's wife took a liking to Joseph. She was after his affections and when he resisted her, she betrayed him. After being falsely accused of attempting to rape her, he was thrown into prison. Again, this was another great opportunity for bitterness. Here he was, once again being punished for no apparent reason, in prison on a false accusation without a trial. What injustice! How unfair! Where is the ACLU when you need them?

Anyway, again we see a man whom God prospered in a bad situation. I believe, by now, Joseph had come to the belief that only God could be trusted. Genesis 39:21 says: *"But the LORD was with Joseph and showed him mercy, and He gave him favor in the sight of the keeper of the prison."* Joseph understood his need for God and knew what it took to stay in that place of faith regardless of circumstances.

Even in prison, God prospered him. Through the process of time and some well-placed dream interpretations, Joseph was brought before Pharaoh. After wisely interpreting Pharaoh's dreams, with God's help, Joseph was elevated to the number two position in Egypt, second only to Pharaoh himself. Joseph was now free.

Now we come to an important point. If you continually put your faith and trust in God, He will always come through. Although you may not always understand the reason that He allows certain things to happen, you must still keep your focus on God and His plan for you. Joseph would soon learn the purpose of all of his trials.

I am convinced that Joseph had given all things up to God. You can see it in his actions. For instance, look at the names he gave to his children: Manasseh, which means forgetting, "For God has made me forget all my toil and all of my father's house," and Ephraim, which means fruitful, "For God has caused me to be fruitful in the land of my affliction." I again want to state that this does not look like a man who was ruled by bitterness, but a man of great faith in God.

The time came when a great famine had broken out in all the land, as foretold through the interpretation of Pharaoh's dream. Operating according to the wisdom that God had given to Joseph, Pharaoh had managed to acquire all of the wealth, grain, livestock, and land in Egypt. By following Joseph's counsel, Pharaoh was now the most powerful man in the region. This news made its way to Jacob in Canaan. Since the famine was there also, he sent his sons, except for Benjamin, to go to Egypt and buy food. The brothers then, without knowing it, came face to face with Joseph. If you read the story and only look at the surface, what happens next could be seen as an attempt at some payback. What Joseph did to his brothers certainly has the appearance of torment. But, look closer, Joseph always wept and showed great compassion any time he dealt with his brothers. I believe God was in charge of this entire exchange and Joseph was simply doing what he sensed that God wanted him to do.

The end result says it all. God needed to get Jacob and his entire family to a place where they could survive the famine and eventually grow to become the great people that He had promised to Abraham. If God had left them in Canaan, some or all of them might have starved out. Instead, the entire family was preserved. If Joseph was still harboring resentment, I don't think God could have used him. But, as history now shows, Jacob did survive and the nation of Israel was preserved.

What this shows me is that the fruit of forgiveness is salvation. If Joseph had not been walking in forgiveness, he could have easily destroyed his family. He could have used his power to make life very miserable for his brothers, even making them his slaves. That didn't happen. The Israelites prospered and had peace all of the days of Joseph. They found great favor with Pharaoh and were granted the best land in which to dwell. It wasn't until after both Joseph and that Pharaoh had died that the people were enslaved, which was a direct result of the new Pharaoh's fear of their great prosperity. The point here is to let God be the minister of justice. When we surrender that to God, we can then be used by God to affect His plans, maybe save our own family or a future nation.

David and Absalom
Much has been written to describe David. He was a shepherd and a king, the sweet psalmist of Israel and a mighty warrior. Best of all, he was a man after God's own heart. David was truly an amazing man.

David also exhibited the attributes of a man of forgiveness. He almost always chose God over self. David wasn't perfect by any means. He had his flaws, and there was that Bathsheba incident, but doing what was right before God was still his driving passion. Even in his failings, he always seemed to find his way into God's grace. He understood when to fight and when to surrender.

David was also a man of great faith. He trusted in God to provide and to deliver him from peril. He was not a man of vengeance, but a man of great purpose. Whether he was tending the sheep or fighting giants, he always had God in mind, looking for God's hand to move.

David also showed the ability to not retain offense. When he was being pursued by King Saul, who had nothing but evil in mind for him, David remained humble. He would not strike out at Saul nor would he rise up to overtake him. He recognized that Saul was God's anointed and therefore was God's problem to deal with.

David's heart was to forgive Saul, even though he had every right to defend himself and even take over. God had already told David that he would be king. Samuel had even anointed him. So David had justification to go after Saul when it was apparent that Saul had it in for him. But, he didn't. Instead, he humbled himself and let God be God. He trusted God to make good on His word and David was delivered. David did not show malice towards Saul and even went so far as to defend him. As David moved in this way, God did eventually elevate him to be king. By David's faith and trust in God, he became a great king.

Possibly one of the greatest examples of David's compassion and love came when his son, Absalom, chose to commit great wrongs against David and his family. David had many sons and daughters. Second Samuel 13 recounts the story of Amnon and Tamar, two of David's children. Amnon had a different mother than Tamar and Absalom. Amnon became obsessed with his half-sister, Tamar, and desired to have her. Initially, it appeared that he was in love with her, but, through his deceitful heart, that love turned to lust. He devised a plan to get her alone with him in his bedroom, and then he raped her. After this happened, he threw her out and despised her. With her honor tainted, she ran away. Upon hearing of this, David became very angry, although the Bible is silent on what his actions were. Absalom heard of it also, but his actions were quite clear. He waited for the right moment, and then devised a plan to kill Amnon. Absalom harbored the bitterness of the offense against his sister and took matters into his own hands. It is said that revenge is best served cold, and in cold blood, Amnon was murdered.

Absalom then fled to another land to escape the king's wrath. David was greatly upset by all of this. The loss of Amnon, together with Tamar's shame and Absalom's flight, left him deeply saddened. Second Samuel 13:37-39 shows David's sorrow and that he deeply missed Absalom. *"But Absalom fled and went to Talmai the son of Ammihud, king of Geshur. And David mourned for his son every day. So Absalom fled and went to Geshur, and was there three years. And King David longed to go to Absalom. For he had been comforted concerning Amnon, because he was dead."* This doesn't sound like someone who is lying in wait for retribution but more like a loving father longing for his son. Granted, evil had been done and punishment was due by the law. There were no innocent parties here, except maybe for Tamar.

How many times do we see families today being torn apart by strife and revenge? What Amnon did was clearly wrong, and justice was deserved. What Absalom did was also equally wrong. It seems to me that the fruit of unforgiveness is destruction and sorrow. There has been much debate over what David should have done. Clearly he didn't follow his responsibility here, but that is a discussion for another day. What I want to draw attention to is the different attitudes shown by David and Absalom. David was a man of humility and restraint. He could have, with the wave of his hand, had Absalom destroyed, but he didn't. His choice was to love his son. He eventually allowed Absalom's return. In 2 Samuel 14, we even see the beginning of a restoration process. Absalom, however, was an arrogant man, full of bitterness. He eventually succumbed to his pride and rose up and take his father's throne. He launched another conspiracy and eventually chased David out. In a bold move, he won the hearts of many people and took the kingdom. David ran for his life, but still did not rise up to take matters into his own hands. Eventually Absalom, acting on faulty counsel, moved to eliminate David completely.

David was now very old, and I am sure he was tired of running. He had been thoroughly embarrassed and run out of town. If ever there was a time to get angry and plot revenge, this would be it. But an amazing thing happened as David gave the order to retake the kingdom. He said to go easy on the young man Absalom. He didn't want his head on a platter or some great form of torture to be performed. He wasn't out for revenge. Maybe it was just the delusion of old age, or maybe David just knew what he must do to please God. After all, it was God who had put David in as king in the first place. I believe David had knowledge of God's desire for forgiveness and that God would render judgment.

Of course, judgment was administered and Absalom was killed. But even in the end, David wept at the news of his son's death. Furthermore, David did not strike down Joab for his treachery in killing Absalom. He simply removed him from his position of authority. In doing these things, I believe David remained faithful to God.

Lewis B. Smedes writes in his book, *Forgive and Forget: Healing the Hurts We Don't Deserve,* "The problem with revenge is that it never gets what it wants; it never evens the score. Fairness never comes. The chain reaction set off by every act of vengeance always takes its unhindered course. It ties both the injured and the injurer to the escalator of pain…" We must not get caught up in the tit-for-tat revenge game.

In the end, David was restored as king and his line was preserved. Remember, the fruit of unforgiveness is destruction while the fruit of forgiveness is salvation.

The Key Of Forgiveness-

Chapter 4

Jesus' Teaching on Forgiveness

"This is My beloved Son. Hear Him!"
— *God Luke 9:35*

The above quote was spoken by God to Peter, James and John. I think it would be wise for us to do so as well. Up to this point, I have written about my opinion regarding forgiveness. Let's now follow what God said and focus our attention on Jesus' words. In order to properly examine what Jesus said, you must first consider the role forgiveness played in His ministry. Jesus came into the world with the singular purpose of redeeming mankind to God. Since man was separated from God by sin, forgiveness of sin was the driving need. I think it is safe to say that Jesus' entire ministry was based on man's absolute need for forgiveness. With that in mind, I want to explore some different passages of the Bible and look at what was taught.

In Matthew 7:1 and 2, Jesus says, *"Judge not, that you be not judged. For with what judgment you judge, you will be judged; and with the measure you use, it will be measured back to you."* Passing judgment on one another is a very common trap that we fall into. Jesus is showing us here that there needs to be great care used in how we critically view each other. As these verses clearly show, judgmental actions toward others can have a profound effect on us. There is a saying in life that goes like this: "What goes around comes around." As this applies to forgiveness, I suppose you could say, "With the measure of forgiveness you use, it will be measured back to you." This is a common theme in what Jesus taught.

In Luke 7, Jesus makes a very powerful point to a Pharisee named Simon. Jesus had been invited into Simon's house for a meal. As he sat down at the table, He was approached by a woman who apparently was of questionable reputation. With a great display of humility, she proceeded to wash Jesus' feet with her tears and dry his feet with her hair, kissing them the whole time. She then broke an alabaster flask of fragrant oil and anointed His feet with it. As all of this was happening, Simon was thinking, *"This Man, if He were a prophet, would know who and what manner of woman this is who is touching*

Him, for she is a sinner." Jesus knew his thoughts and responded to Simon as follows: *"Simon, I have something to say to you."* So he said, *"Teacher, say it." "There was a certain creditor who had two debtors. One owed five hundred denarii, and the other fifty. And when they had nothing with which to repay, he freely forgave them both. Tell Me, therefore, which of them will love him more?"* Simon answered and said, *"I suppose the one whom he forgave more."* And He said to him, *"You have rightly judged."* Then He turned to the woman and said to Simon, *"Do you see this woman? I entered your house; you gave Me no water for My feet, but she has washed My feet with her tears and wiped them with the hair of her head."* You gave Me no kiss, but this woman has not ceased to kiss My feet since the time I came in. You did not anoint My head with oil, but this woman has anointed My feet with fragrant oil. Therefore I say to you, her sins, which are many, are forgiven, for she loved much. But to whom little is forgiven, the same loves little."* Then He said to her, *"Your sins are forgiven."*

I am sure this was an uncomfortable moment for Simon and all who were present. Jesus was drawing a sharp contrast between the humility of the woman and the arrogance of the Pharisee. While doing so, He revealed to us His greater purpose, the forgiveness of sins. This passage also shows the relationship between forgiveness and love. This is important to see. The Bible says that the world will know we are Christians by our love for one another. If we are not actively forgiving people, how much love will be seen in us?

In John 20:23, Jesus tells us, *"If you forgive the sins of any, they are forgiven: if you retain the sins of any, they are retained."* Here again is the concept shown in the Matthew 7 passages. It also begins to establish the idea of being bound together by sin. Clearly, being bound together by sin or offenses cannot be a good thing.

In Matthew 6:14 and 15, Jesus established another important truth. *"If you forgive men their trespasses, your heavenly father will also forgive you. But, if you do not forgive men their trespasses, neither will your father forgive your trespasses."* This is possibly one of the most disturbing teachings Jesus gave on forgiveness. This is not simply a one-time statement that can be open for interpretation. Jesus states it again in the Lord's Prayer — *"And forgive us our debts AS we forgive our debtors."* No matter how you say it, we are asking in prayer for God to be conditional in His forgiveness toward us. Again, this is a very frightening concept. Our inability, or lack of willingness, to forgive can cause God not to forgive. I know this appears to conflict with the message of grace, but this is what Jesus taught so we must take heed. While I do believe that grace is extended to us, as believers we must follow what Jesus taught. This all leads me to believe that Jesus' intention was for us to live a life of forgiveness, period.

In my opinion, the definitive teaching on forgiveness is found in Matthew 18. Through the ages much has been taught and discussed regarding this chapter. In the first several verses of this chapter, Jesus discusses humility. He says we need to be like little children. Children have the most amazing capacity to trust and forgive. When my oldest daughter was just a toddler, we were in Seattle for a conference. There were several days of meetings which, when they were over, left her tired and cranky. At the end of one of the evening meetings, she was brought to me in tears. She had had enough of what was going on and needed some "daddy time." As I picked her up, she settled down into my arms. Before long she was sound asleep. As I looked at her, I saw a beautiful picture. This child of mine had so much trust in me that she knew she could fall asleep in my arms and be completely safe. At that moment, for her, all was well. I do believe this is how God wants us to view Him — to have the ability to trust Him like a little child. There is much we can learn from that.

In the next few verses, Jesus talks about offenses. He warns us not to offend the little children, as well as not to sin. In Matthew 18:15-17, He teaches us how to deal with an offending brother. *"Moreover if your brother sins against you, go and tell him his fault between you and him alone. If he hears you, you have gained your brother. But if he will not hear, take with you one or two more, that 'by the mouth of two or three witnesses every word may be established.' And if he refuses to hear them, tell it to the church. But if he refuses even to hear the church, let him be to you like a heathen and a tax collector."*

I feel that many times people will use this passage as a justification to render quick judgment. It is here where our pride can become a real stumbling block to forgiveness. I believe that Jesus' desire was for us to make people aware of the hurt they caused while giving them the opportunity to correct the problem. But too often this time is used to level accusation. It is seen as a way to bring a person into a unilateral admission of guilt. If our pride is not checked here, we will most likely miss the chance to admit our own contribution to the problem. If we are not humble, as Jesus taught earlier, we could ruin any chance of reconciliation.

Far too often we get in a hurry and prematurely move on to step two, witnesses. In the quest for vindication, there seems to be a frequent desire to involve others in the process. There are some very legitimate times for this step, as well as step three (to bring it before the church), but I am convinced that if we are able to remain humble and to completely trust God, the need for these steps can be avoided. Of course, if the person that is being confronted is operating in open sin or promoting a blatantly heretical doctrine, then that must be dealt with accordingly. It is vital for the well-being of the church that proper order be observed. The issues I am referring to are the more personal problems we face with each other — the general disagreements and arguments that many times lead to bitter divisions and hurts. To put it another way, it is the basic failure to communicate. In this regard, I believe it would be both easier, as well as more profitable, to simply swallow our pride and get over it.

Many offenses arise over little disagreements about how or what is the best or right way to do something. This kind of behavior can have devastating effects, of which I have even seen in our church. Through the years, a number of disputes have arisen, just like what happens anywhere. Unfortunately, they ended with times of discord and division. During the late 1980s, a dispute arose within leadership that spilled out into the general congregation. Many people were caught up in the "he said this, he said that" game. As people staked out their "turf," the anger built and tension grew. Finally, it came to the point of eruption in 1992, splitting the church in two. Many people were devastated by this; some scattered, and some are no longer serving God. It was a sad time, and the bitterness and hurt lasted for several years.

As pride mixes with anger and confusion, damage will occur. When these types of situations arise, the reconciliation process can only begin at the point of forgiveness. Christian author, Dr. Stephen Crosby made this statement: "A mature Christian has the capacity to absorb the offenses and weakness of others, not just demand that they perform up to the code of ideals." For some people, though, this was just too much to handle.

Thankfully, our church recovered and is now vibrant and growing. We have come to learn the importance of forgiving and it has led to significant restoration. Relationships that were shattered have been repaired, and many people that had left have returned. Unfortunately, many of those who were hurt still remain estranged. By maintaining a forgiving attitude, we can learn to remain in complete unity without having to agree on every little detail.

In Matthew 18:18, Jesus introduces another important idea. *"Assuredly, I say to you, whatever you bind on earth will be bound in heaven, and whatever you loose on earth will be loosed in heaven."* It is important to understand that we have the power to bind up or loosen things, including offenses. As I was praying for insight about this, God revealed to me this thought: We can bind ourselves together with a cord of offense. Imagine someone doing something to hurt or offend you. Maybe it was a harmless prank or possibly an unfounded accusation. Whatever the cause, you are now mad. You approach them and discuss it with them, yet even though you follow what the scriptures say to do, you do not feel satisfied with the results. You now have a choice, hold on to it or release it. If you choose not to forgive, you will be left bound together by that offense. Every time you see or think of that individual, all you will remember is the wrong that was done. It will possibly cloud all of your judgments or actions towards that person, hindering any possible chance for reconciliation. I understand this because I have had to deal with this myself. You pray for God to intervene and do something about it, but nothing happens. Why? It is not just bound on earth, but also in heaven. The problem here is not God or even the other person, it is now you. God will not violate your free will. He gave you the right to make choices and holds you to them. If you choose to bind something, it is bound. The only way to move away from it is another choice — to forgive.

Remember, when you forgive, you are RELEASING the binding of a contract. When you choose not to forgive, you are deciding to stay bound by that contract. By not forgiving, you are literally telling God that your choice is to stay involved in whatever the problem was that caused the strife in the first place. By binding it here, you are, in effect, putting a restraining order on God. It is a matter of putting your own will in front of God's will. The end result of this is always bitterness, envy, strife, anger, hatred... I think you get the point. If not, you need to read Galatians 5:19-21. Paul lists the works of the flesh. *"Now the works of the flesh are evident, which are: adultery, fornication, uncleanness, lewdness, idolatry, sorcery, hatred, contentions, jealousies, outbursts of wrath, selfish ambitions, dissensions, heresies, envy, murders, drunkenness, revelries, and the like; of which I tell you beforehand, just as I also told you in time past, that those who practice such things will not inherit the kingdom of God."* It's a disturbing list.

In Matthew 18:22, Peter asks Jesus a very interesting question: *"Lord, how often shall my brother sin against me and I forgive him? Up to seven times?"* This is a fair question. To our flesh nature, forgiving someone seven times for the same offense is being very gracious, but when is enough, enough? Jesus responded by saying, *"I do not say to you up to seven times, but up to seventy times seven."* In other words, always. He isn't setting a restriction on forgiveness. Instead, he is giving us an extreme charge that requires even more humility. In fact, Jesus is possibly implying that by forgiving over and over, you are actually setting yourself up for more trouble. It is here that, if God truly is to be our vindicator, we are going to have to trust Him. By setting no limits on the forgiveness to be extended, Jesus is forcing us to absolutely lean on God's mercy.

Jesus then teaches the parable of the unforgiving servant in Matthew 18:24-34: *"Therefore the kingdom of heaven is like a certain king who wanted to settle accounts with his servants. And when he had begun to settle accounts, one was brought to him who owed him ten thousand talents. But as he was not able to pay, his master commanded that he be sold, with his wife and children and all that he had, and that payment be made. The servant therefore fell down before him, saying, 'Master, have patience with me, and I will pay you all.' Then the master of that servant was moved with compassion, released him, and forgave him the debt. But that servant went out and found one of his fellow servants who owed* him a hundred denarii; and he laid hands on him and took him by the throat, saying, 'Pay me what you owe!' So his fellow servant fell down at his feet and begged him, saying, 'Have patience with me, and I will pay you all.' And he would not, but went and threw him into prison till he should pay the debt. So when his fellow servants saw what had been done, they were very grieved, and came and told their master all that had been done. Then his master, after he had called him, said to him, 'You wicked servant! I forgave you all that debt because you begged me. Should you not also have had compassion on your fellow servant, just as I had pity on you?' And his master was angry, and delivered him to the torturers until he should pay all that was due to him."*

The master revoked his forgiveness. If that does not disturb you, then read verse 35: *"So my heavenly Father also will do if each of you, from his heart, does not forgive his brother his trespasses."*

Wow! God will not forgive us if we do not forgive others. How else can you read that? It is very clear to me that we are commanded to forgive. Let me give you another way to view this. You must not only forgive the action, but the actor. This happens in the heart. When you forgive what was done but not who did it, you leave yourself open to continually blame that individual. It shows up in your actions. If you see someone who has hurt you in the past and you refuse to interact with them, your forgiveness toward them is suspect. This is used as a defense mechanism, trying to "protect" ourselves from some future hurt that might be caused. By doing this, you are literally saying, "Your past ACTIONS are forgiven, but since I am sure you will do it again, YOU are not." Jesus gave us an additional warning in Matthew 5:21 and 22: *"You have heard that it was said to those of old, 'You shall not murder, and whoever murders will be in danger of the judgment.' But I say to you that whoever is angry with his brother without a cause shall be in danger of the judgment."* We must learn that to forgive is from the heart, not just the head. If we forgive the act, we must also forgive the actor.

As I have meditated on this parable, another interesting thought developed. It was only after the other servants saw the actions of the first servant, and reported them to the master, that the master revoked his forgiveness. We know that we have an adversary, the devil, who goes about looking for whom he might destroy. We know that the devil is the accuser of the brethren. I can see Satan going before God and laying out his case regarding our unwillingness to forgive, after we have been forgiven all. Since this would be a new and current transgression and a willful disobedience of God's command, how will God respond? If I am reading this passage correctly, it certainly looks bad for the person who holds unforgiveness in his or her heart. Again, I do not want to get into an argument about the law of grace, but it is very clear what Jesus is teaching here. If we don't forgive, God won't forgive.

Why is this important? Why did Jesus make such a big deal out of forgiving each other? Isn't it God's job to forgive and our job to simply believe? If the world is to know we are Christians by our love for one another, yet we keep holding on to offenses and allowing bitterness and envy to be present, how much love will really be seen? This is not a very good witness to the love and grace of God, is it? We must forgive each other so that the world can truly see the real love of God in us. Only then will we be able to freely share this love with them

THE KEY OF FORGIVENESS-

Chapter 5

Binding and Loosing

"When you hold resentment toward one another, you are bound to that person or condition by an emotional link that is stronger than steel. Forgiveness is the only way to dissolve that link and get free."
    — *Cathleen Ponder, Inspirational Author*

In the previous chapter, I mentioned the binding and loosing concept. In this chapter I want to examine closely how this can actually affect us.

Have you ever been hurt or offended by someone? Of course, the answer is yes, we all have. It is a real part of life that when certain things happen, we become angry. Sometimes it is something big, like infidelity in marriage or serious physical abuse. Other times it is relatively small, like a silly argument over what color to paint the bedroom. Either way, we end up miffed. It is how we respond that is important. We all want to have things resolved and worked out for the best. The problem arises when we can't agree on what "the best" is. It is here that pride enters in, where the need to be right overrides the need for truth. It's a danger zone for all sorts of bitterness and resentment. This is where the most damage is done to relationships. God has a better way, through forgiveness, but our simple human nature generally seems to win out and into the abyss we go. Why? How is it that we choose to trust God with our health, finances, even our soul, but when it comes to the need for vindication, we choose to trust ourselves?

I can honestly say that I, again, speak from experience. Many times in my life I have gone through trials and troubles that left me wounded and angry. I went looking for a way to make things right, only to find myself sunk deep in the mire of bitterness and outright depression. Always the end result was loss in some form or another. But, as I have grown in the knowledge of God, I have begun to learn why this happens, and have seen how God's way is infinitely better.

In Matthew 16:19 and 18:18, Jesus said, *"What you bind on earth is bound in Heaven and what you loose on Earth is loosed in Heaven."* This is most profound when it comes to offenses.

Imagine being tied to a tree in a hurricane. The wind is whipping and rain is pounding, yet nothing can be done to stop it from tearing you apart. Now consider this: instead of seeking shelter when you knew the storm was on its way, you chose instead to tie yourself to a tree, refusing to let go as the storm hit. The damage you sustained was largely self-inflicted, as your pleas for God to save you went unanswered. In the end you are battered and bruised, with a new-found anger at God. After all, He didn't answer your cries for help. Of course, you could have avoided all of it by just releasing yourself from that tree, and then safely getting into the shelter before it was too late.

That is how unforgiveness works. We bind ourselves to someone by a cord of offense, then refuse to let go. Maybe it's a friend or a family member, or possibly someone at work or even in the church. Every time you see or think of them, you become upset. As the bitterness sets in, it begins to affect your relationships with other people. You are now starting to have difficulty trusting others. As things progress, you look to involve others in the ordeal. You might even go so far as to implicate the original person as the source of all of your troubles.

In the midst of all of this, you cry out to God to heal your bitterness and to restore peace in your life, all the while praying for God's will to be done in the offender's life. This prayer, of course, is just a veiled attempt to try to convince God to mete out some form of punishment on that person for the great wrong they have done to you. But when God doesn't respond, a greater level of frustration sets in and deeper into the hole of despair you fall. You seek counsel, therapy, maybe even mood management drugs, but nothing works. Eventually your bitterness extends toward God, even causing you to consider giving up on Him all together. Maybe you don't go to that extreme but instead just try to bury the feelings deep and go about your business as if nothing was ever wrong. But then it only takes one little thing to set you off and you are right back where you started. Even time won't make it go away.

Why? What you bound is bound! You have bound yourself to the tree of offense with your own hands, and you never let go. Somewhere in the process, you chose not to forgive the person whom you felt wronged you. Maybe it was just a simple disagreement or an unresolved argument, but you chose to retain it and therefore bound it up. And, of course, you didn't just bind it here on earth, but also in Heaven. Remember, God will never violate your will. It's up to you to submit your will to God. If you choose to bind yourself to something and not let go, God is not going to forcibly tear you from it. He will honor your desire to stay bound. The trouble really comes when you bind yourself with unforgiveness. At that point, you are literally binding yourself to sin, as that is what unforgiveness really is. Sin is the contract with the devil that leads to death. Although that contract was paid in full by Jesus at the cross, if you choose to again bind yourself to it through the sin of unforgiveness, God is bound to leave you there.

God wants us to always trust Him fully. This means in all aspects of our lives. If we choose to retain or bind an offense, we are actually telling God that we don't want or need His help in dealing with the situation. It is our pride that causes us to believe that God must need our help in order to resolve the issue. For some insane reason, we can't see how God can possibly make it all right, without our involvement. Yet our involvement is the first thing God wants removed.

God gave me an interesting revelation once during a very stressful time when I was involved in a dispute with someone in the church. Things had become rather tense. At the height of the situation, as I was praying for an answer, God told me I had to release it and get out of His way or He could not fully shine His light on the problem. He then showed me that I was like a large tree, casting a shadow. God wanted to fully expose something with His light, but I was in the way. I was preventing Him from doing what He wanted to do. I had to be literally removed from the line of God's light. What I saw was that as I retained the problem, I was blocking Him. As I bound myself to the issue, He was bound from it. I had to forgive before God would move. When I finally let go of the situation, God moved and the problem was resolved in a very positive manner. I had to forgive the person, not because I was right or that there had been some form of repentance, but because I was blocking God from His desired purpose. By forgiving unconditionally, I subdued my pride. Only then was God free to work.

That's the beauty of God's way, and it always works out best for God. If it is best for God, it has to be best for us, too. By my letting go, I was able to find safe shelter in God, thus avoiding the storm. Because I didn't receive the storm's damage, I was spared the bitterness and strife. The end result was a complete restoration with that person and peace in my soul. Remember, what you bind is bound, and what you loose is loosed.

Chapter 6

The Most Powerful Spiritual Weapon

"The weak can never forgive. Forgiveness is the attribute of the strong."
— *Mahatma Gandhi*

Ephesians 6:12 states: *"We do not wrestle against flesh and blood, but against principalities, against powers, against the rulers of darkness of this age, against spiritual hosts of wickedness in the heavenly places."* We are in a spiritual war with a need for powerful weapons in order to prevail. In verse 13, the Apostle Paul says to *"take up the whole armor of God, that you may be able to withstand in the evil day..."*

We all know that you never want to go into battle unarmed. Just as armor is a vital defensive tool, a powerful offense is required as well. Winning requires both protection and production.

How does this relate to forgiveness? In the hands of a believer, prayer is a powerful offensive weapon. With prayer, you can communicate your needs directly to God. Through faith you can release the power of God to defeat your spiritual enemies. You can also gain strength through fasting, combined with prayer and faith. Praise and worship are great weapons for tearing down the enemy's strongholds. But I am convinced that the most powerful weapon available is forgiveness.

Forgiveness is the key that unlocks the door to a powerful faith. Without it, our prayers may be blocked, or go unheard. If our faith is weak or our prayers are blocked, we may see defeat. By releasing the power of forgiveness, we can stand strong in the presence of God, allowing our faith to be fully charged, and our prayers heard. Without faith, it is impossible to please God, yet with weak faith it is impossible to experience the fullness of God's pleasure for us.

Jesus' ministry was emphasized by forgiveness and reconciliation. In Matthew 5:23 and 24, He spoke of this by telling us to reconcile with people before bringing an offering to the altar. In Mark 11:25 and 26, Jesus teaches: *"And whenever you stand praying, if you have anything against anyone, forgive him, that your Father in heaven may also forgive you your trespasses. But if you do not forgive, neither will your Father in heaven forgive your trespasses."* Again, you can see that forgiveness comes first. This is important to unlocking faith.

Sin will separate us from God. Unforgiveness is a sin. So it is clear that we must forgive or risk being separated from God. When we forgive others, God then forgives us, opening up the channels to a powerful faith. Something else happens when we forgive — it sets us free from the bond of sin. This is important since the bond of sin is Satan's hold on us.

When Adam sinned in the garden, he handed his legal authority over to Satan. Thus sin created a legal bond over us and ultimately produced death. Forgiveness is the key to being released from that bond. The greatest display of this power came at the cross.

Jesus lived a sinless life, passing all of the tests and overcoming all temptations. Many times during his ministry he was looked upon with contempt by the religious leaders, even branded a blasphemer and told that he was of Beelzebub, lord of the demons. Never once striking back with anger, He instead prayed for people, seeking to bring them into the Kingdom of God. All of this was done in accordance with the Father's desire. Still there was something left to be done, the sacrifice.

As a sinless man, Jesus alone was worthy to be that sacrifice. For mankind to be fully redeemed, Jesus had to shed His blood and die to pay the price for all sin. While He willingly went to His death, fulfilling His destiny by taking upon Himself the sins of all humanity, it was on the cross that He passed His greatest test.

This was a brutal time for Jesus. He knew that to have all sins placed on Him meant that His Father had to forsake and separate from Him, since God cannot coexist with sin. As a man, apart from His Father, Jesus performed His greatest act: forgiving us. As He said, *"Father, forgive them for they know not what they do,"* He was able to loose Himself from the bond of sin. He remained a pure and sinless man. Since He could not be charged with the sin of unforgiveness, death had no authority over Him. As He gave up His spirit and died, He paid the final price for all of us, thus making salvation available for those who choose to believe. In doing this, He also set a standard we all must follow.

Imagine, for a moment, the extreme pain and suffering Jesus experienced. Having been betrayed by one of His closest followers, He was then falsely accused, tried, and sentenced to death by crucifixion. After being beaten into an unrecognizable condition, He was nailed to the cross. Jesus was ridiculed, spat on, tormented and cursed, all while suffering what has been considered to be one of the most excruciating deaths possible. I have to ask, how many of us would be in a loving and forgiving mood at this point? Realize that was only Jesus' physical reality. In the midst of His greatest pain, His Father had to reject, turn and forsake Him. Jesus was then left, as a man, on the cross to bear it all, alone. Add to this the weight of all of the world's sin and sickness, as well as pure spiritual torment from the demons….. check please.

Then, at the point of His greatest struggle, He said, "Father, forgive them." As this was happening, heaven and hell shook. Although the devil was certain that he had won, Jesus, who remained sinless, was the ultimate victor. He took back all of the authority that Adam had surrendered and brought redemption to all mankind. If Jesus had not forgiven everything, He would have sinned and all would have been lost.

Forgiveness is the one weapon Satan has no answer for. He cannot duplicate or counter it. It is the ultimate act of selflessness. When we forgive others, God forgives us. The responsibility is placed squarely on our shoulders, setting us up to sink or swim by our own actions.

To fully be in the center of the will of God, we must be fully surrendered to the will of God. If we choose to retain offenses, we are placing a barrier of self will between us and God. This makes complete surrender impossible.

As I said before, forgiveness is the most powerful weapon we have available. It causes us to lay down our self will and allows us to be guided by God's will. In that place, I believe the devil has no power over us, as he had no power over Jesus. We must learn to forgive to win.

Chapter 7

Stephen and Paul

"Forgiveness is the remission of sins. For it is by this that what has been lost, and was found, is saved from being lost again."
— *Saint Augustine of Hippo (396-430 A.D.)*

The New Testament has examples of people who demonstrated how to live a life of forgiveness. In Acts 6 we meet one of them — Stephen.

Stephen was one of seven men chosen by the apostles to serve the church as a deacon. Acts 6:8 says of him: *"And Stephen, full of faith and power, did great wonders and signs among the people."*

He was a vigorous defender of the faith, and by the wisdom of the Holy Spirit he debated the religious rulers concerning Jesus. After masterfully presenting the truth of the gospel, with many scriptural references, he was condemned as a blasphemer. When his words of truth had cut the people to their hearts, they decided to stone him to death. Acts 7:54-60 describes this incident and introduces us to the other person I want to discuss, Paul. *"When they heard these things they were cut to the heart, and they gnashed at him with their teeth. But he, being full of the Holy Spirit, gazed into heaven and saw the glory of God, and Jesus standing at the right hand of God, and said, "Look! I see the heavens opened and the Son of Man standing at the right hand of God!" Then they cried out with a loud voice, stopped their ears, and ran at him with one accord; and they cast him out of the city and stoned him. And the witnesses laid down their clothes at the feet of a young man named Saul. And they stoned Stephen as he was calling on God and saying, "Lord Jesus, receive my spirit." Then he knelt down and cried out with a loud voice, "Lord, do not charge them with this sin." And when he had said this, he fell asleep."*

Stephen gave his life as a martyr for the gospel of Jesus Christ. He clearly understood the need for forgiveness and, like Jesus, Stephen chose to forgive those who were causing him harm. I believe this was his way of living, not just an isolated incident. Stephen was a man who was full of the Spirit of God. He had no apparent hindrances to his prayers, seeing that he performed great works. His forgiveness also displayed his tremendous faith. Stephen trusted God, right up to his death, knowing that whatever happened, he was in God's hands. By forgiving those who were killing him, he was a great witness to the love of God.

Paul
Stephen didn't hold offense, even at the point of death. I believe this act must have had some impact on the young man, Saul. Although Saul consented to Stephen's death, and afterward began actively persecuting the church, God was working on him.

We meet up with him again in Acts 9. This chapter describes Saul's conversion. I believe Saul's encounters with the people that he was persecuting were starting to have an affect on him. Saul was, after all, a man who sought after righteousness, truly longing to serve God. In verses 3 through 6, Saul personally encountered Jesus while on a mission to round up Christians and incarcerate them: *"As he journeyed he came near Damascus, and suddenly a light shone around him from heaven. Then he fell to the ground, and heard a voice saying to him, "Saul, Saul, why are you persecuting Me?" And he said, "Who are You, Lord?" Then the Lord said, "I am Jesus, whom you are persecuting. It is hard for you to kick against the goads." So he, trembling and astonished, said, "Lord, what do You want me to do?" Then the Lord said to him, "Arise and go into the city, and you will be told what you must do."* Saul was converted. He realized who Jesus was and, trembling, he humbled himself and his new life began.

Saul, who later was to be known as Paul, became a great apostle. He was responsible for introducing the gospel to many nations, planting and leading numerous churches. He was the writer of most of the New Testament, and gave us some of the greatest messages on grace, love, and righteousness. He was also heavily persecuted, and endured being mocked, beaten, stoned, imprisoned, tortured, and ultimately martyred. This provided him ample opportunities to develop a bad attitude. It would have been easy for him to have grown bitter against those who caused him harm, yet he wasn't bitter. Instead, he considered all of these trials as nothing compared to the love of God in his life. Throughout his writings, he is seen constantly praying for blessings to come upon people. Tremendous love and compassion marked his life. His heart can be seen through his teachings.

In Philippians 2:1-4, Paul wrote about humility: *"Therefore if there is any consolation in Christ, if any comfort of love, if any fellowship of the Spirit, if any affection and mercy, fulfill my joy by being like-minded, having the same love, being of one accord, of one mind. Let nothing be done through selfish ambition or conceit, but in lowliness of mind let each esteem others better than himself. Let each of you look out not only for his own interests, but also for the interests of others."* This shows the heart of a forgiving life. Paul had no selfish ambitions but honored others above himself.

A modern-day saint who embodied this principle was Mother Teresa. She exemplified a lifetime of selfless service, always putting the needs of others before her own. She once shared one of her prayers: "Sweetest Lord, make me appreciative of the dignity of my high vocation, and its many responsibilities. Never permit me to disgrace it by giving way to coldness, unkindness, or impatience." People will do things that disappoint you, but by continually placing the needs of others first, it becomes easier to forgive them when they stumble. Being humble allows God to move on your behalf. Paul lived this way. He didn't regard what was happening to him as anything to harbor bitterness over, instead he just called them "light afflictions" (2 Corinthians 4:17).

Paul moved in great power. He healed the sick, raised the dead, and even survived many potentially fatal incidents. He was shipwrecked and bitten by a snake, yet showed no ill effects. God was clearly with him, always. Paul taught us about love and grace. I do not believe he could have done all of this without being a man with complete faith and trust in God. If he were prone to unforgiveness, I think it would have shown up in his work.

He did issue warnings about bad behavior and sinful living, but he also encouraged reconciliation in the end. In 2 Corinthians 2:5-11, he wrote: *"But if anyone has caused grief, he has not grieved me, but all of you to some extent--not to be too severe. This punishment which was inflicted by the majority is sufficient for such a man, so that, on the contrary, you ought rather to forgive and comfort him, lest perhaps such a one be swallowed up with too much sorrow. Therefore I urge you to reaffirm your love to him. For to this end I also wrote, that I might put you to the test, whether you are obedient in all things. Now whom you forgive anything, I also forgive. For if indeed I have forgiven anything, I have forgiven that one for your sakes in the presence of Christ, lest Satan should take advantage of us; for we are not ignorant of his devices."* This passage was a follow-up to a rebuke written in 1 Corinthians, where he administered discipline for a terrible immoral sin that was being tolerated in the church. His instruction was for the people to separate themselves from the offender. It was necessary to isolate the offender in order to keep the church pure and the people free of the influence of that sin. Later, as he saw the potential for rejection of the offender's repentance, Paul instructed the people to forgive. How often do we confront, then arbitrarily cut someone off from fellowship, never acknowledging them again? We simply close the door and reject them. How will we know if they have understood the wrong they committed and if they have truly repented if we refuse to reach out and forgive them? The end result of this is well stated by a 19th century psychiatrist named Roberto Assagioli, when he said, "Without forgiveness life is governed by an endless cycle of resentment and retaliation."

Paul instructed us to forgive for the sake of the offender. He had compassion for the man, longing to see him restored to the body out of concern that he might be lost to overwhelming sorrow. We must learn to forgive from the heart. Remember back to the teaching in Matthew 18, Jesus wants restoration, not retaliation. Paul understood this. It is how God operates, so shouldn't we, also? Paul also reminds us of our enemy, Satan. We are not to be ignorant of his ways, nor are we to give him the ammunition to use against us before God. Again, forgiveness is a must.

Possibly one of Paul's most direct teachings on the forgiving life is found in Colossians 3:12 and 13: *"Therefore, as the elect of God, holy and beloved, put on tender mercies, kindness, humility, meekness, longsuffering; bearing with one another, and forgiving one another, if anyone has a complaint against another; even as Christ forgave you, so you also must do."*

In Galatians 5, Paul adds this: *"For you, brethren, have been called to liberty; only do not use liberty as an opportunity for the flesh, but through love serve one another. For all the law is fulfilled in one word, even in this: "You shall love your neighbor as yourself." But if you bite and devour one another, beware lest you be consumed by one another."*

The connection of love and forgiveness is undeniable. We must forgive as Christ forgave. Galatians 5:13 has a stern warning: *"Beware lest you be consumed by one another!"* I think that says it all. Look around at the world we live in. Can you see the damage that's been done by the "works of the flesh?" We are called to be a people set apart for the works of Christ. If we don't learn to live the forgiving life, how will anyone be able to tell us apart from the world?

Chapter 8

The Goats

"Anger will never disappear so long as thoughts of resentment are cherished. Anger will disappear just as soon as thoughts of resentment are forgotten."

— Buddha

I know that seeing a quote from Buddha in a Christian book seems a bit out of place, but I think the statement really helps to make the point of this chapter. I titled it "The Goats" because in this chapter we will be looking at two men whose lives didn't display an understanding of the value of forgiveness — Jonah and Judas.

Jonah

The account of Jonah is an interesting one. Here you have a prophet of God who is called to warn the people of Nineveh of impending doom if they don't repent of their wicked ways. At first, Jonah disobeys and runs from God. After much hardship, he later concedes and does as God had commanded him. Upon receiving the message, Nineveh repents and is spared. Since this is exactly what Jonah had feared would happen, he sits down in frustration and begins to grumble. Jonah was angry with God. He had a deep hatred of the people of Nineveh. They were a brutal people whose evil had reached the heavens. God wanted them destroyed but, due to His justice and compassion, first gave them an opportunity to repent. When He sent Jonah with the message and they responded, God didn't destroy the city. Jonah's anger with God for saving the city was really a show of self pity, like a spoiled child not getting his way.

Jonah understood God's power but not God's love. At one point, Jonah actually showed more concern for a tree than for the people of the city of Nineveh. But in all reality, his concern was likely just for himself. Jonah was unable to forgive the people of Nineveh for the atrocities that they had done to his own people. He wanted them wiped out, and nothing else was acceptable.

God loves us all. When we were all deserving of death, He made a way for us to return to Him. God's desire is for no one to perish. We must be ready to accept that even those people we think are unworthy can be forgiven. It is not up to us to decide who is or isn't worthy of God's grace. Artist and photographer David Ridge said, "True forgiveness is not an action after the fact, it is an attitude with which you enter each moment." Jonah was bitter and selfish. He only would have been happy if the city and the people were destroyed. His bitterness led him to long for death.

This was a serious attitude problem, one that I see in many people today. They receive some form of harm or pick up another's offense and refuse to ever let it go. This leads to long-term bitterness. Like Jonah, they get mad at God when He chooses to bless the ones they believe should be cursed. In their mind, they can't understand why God doesn't punish those who are so obviously deserving of it. But God will not ever arbitrarily punish or destroy anyone. He will always offer a way of repentance to those who are willing to take it. We must never be so self-minded as to expect God to be anything but what He is, just and true. If this understanding cannot be gained, then we risk becoming like Jonah, a bitter, angry person who in the end gets rebuked by God.

Judas
Judas was one of Jesus' chosen disciples. He, like Jonah, had been called by the Lord. But Judas was also a man with selfish ambition. He wanted to see the Romans chased out of Judea and the new King of Israel take over. He was sure that Jesus was the one who would accomplish this. Judas was also a thief, and in the

end was the one who would betray Jesus for thirty pieces of silver.

Let's look at some of the things that Judas did. In John 12:1-6 we get a glimpse of who Judas really was: *"Mary took a pound of very costly oil of spikenard, anointed the feet of Jesus, and wiped His feet with her hair. And the house was filled with the fragrance of the oil. But one of His disciples, Judas Iscariot, Simon's son, who would betray Him, said, "Why was this fragrant oil not sold for three hundred denarii and given to the poor?" This he said, not that he cared for the poor, but because he was a thief, and had the money box; and he used to take what was put in it."* Judas didn't really care for the poor, except maybe poor Judas.

In Matthew 26:14-16, Judas negotiated to betray Jesus: *"Then one of the twelve, called Judas Iscariot, went to the chief priests and said, "What are you willing to give me if I deliver Him to you?" And they counted out to him thirty pieces of silver. So from that time he sought opportunity to betray Him."*

I chose Judas because to me he represents one who could be referred to as an "agenda" person. This kind of individual will usually do things with personal motives, and like Judas they want the end results to be in their own best interests. They can be active in church affairs, saying and doing what appears to be right. But when things don't go as desired, they get upset and attempt to manipulate the situation in their favor. This leads to bitterness and strife. Many times I have seen great works of God derailed over petty personal disputes. It is important to realize what God wants from us. We must always seek to understand His plan and follow His ways. Eighteenth century British statesman, Lord Chesterfield, made an interesting observation: "Wrongs are often forgiven, but contempt never is. Our pride remembers it forever." It is because of our pride that we refuse to let go of things. If living a peaceful and powerful life with God is your goal, forgiving is a must.

Judas had an agenda, and he hated the Romans. His desire was for Jesus to rise up and take the king's throne, and remove the Romans by force. Once it was clear that this wouldn't happen the way he thought it should, Judas took matters into his own hands. Not satisfied with God's plan, he decided to make things happen on his own. In the end, this only brought despair. Judas, too late in realizing his error, ultimately killed himself. This was a tragic ending, and the lesson should be taken seriously. We may not end up dead, in the natural sense, but what about spiritually? A bitter, unforgiving attitude can take you down spiritually, producing a fate worse than death.

I think if we are honest, all of us can relate in some way to Judas. If things don't go our way, we get upset. Sometimes there is dissension, but often we just leave and go our own way. Without resolving things, we just wander. Time after time, place after place, we go looking for peace but don't find it, and we often bring with us much of the trouble we are trying to escape. Without a forgiving attitude, bitterness and dissension grow, eventually causing spiritual death.

At the heart of this problem is unforgiveness. If you go through life in this manner, it will only bring you trouble. Your relationships will be continuously strained and you will never find true freedom in Christ. Russian writer, Leo Tolstoy, said, "Let us forgive each other, only then will we live in peace." I think this is a very wise choice to make.

The title of this chapter is "The Goats." Goats like to butt their heads with everything. I called these two men goats because of their self-serving attitudes. If we want to be truly pleasing to God, we must not be self-serving. Things didn't work out well for Jonah and Judas. Jonah longed to die and Judas killed himself. Choose to live. Choose to forgive.

Chapter 9

Forgive Yourself

"To forgive is to set a prisoner free and discover that the prisoner was you."
— *Lewis B. Smedes, Christian Author (1921-2002)*

Throughout the process of writing this book, I have been constantly challenged to review my own walk in forgiveness. It has involved looking for areas of bitterness I might be harboring towards people in my past. When discovered, the feelings of anger or disappointment had to be dealt with accordingly.

As this occurred, I started to focus on the idea of forgiving myself. It is easy to just say "I forgive myself," but is it as simple as that? How and what do you actually forgive? While pondering this thought, I was taken back to my youth.

Like most teenage boys, I had my share of relationships. Some of these ended decently and some didn't. As a result, I have experienced both the wonder and pain of boy-girl relations. Because this is true for most people, the church I attend stresses a policy of courtship. We try to help our young people avoid the pitfalls of the hook-up then break-up plan known as dating. To a young person already dealing with the stress of becoming an adult, that kind of turmoil can be damaging. Short-term relationships can leave painful emotional scars. Some of the deepest hurts are never resolved, often complicating things later in life.

During my teenage years, I wasn't a Christian. Since I had no solid spiritual guidance, I just went with my feelings. With both natural drive and a desire to not be alone as my guides, I found myself in a few of these ill-fated relationships. These were not all bad, but more often than not they ended up with someone getting hurt. Sometimes I was rejected, but mostly I was the one doing the rejecting. Beyond the initial shock and sadness, I seldom concerned myself with how the other person felt. I would just move on with life and go on my merry way. I know this makes me look like a real jerk, but if you examine life in our world, you will see that this kind of behavior is not all that uncommon. Eventually, God led me to my wife and I have now been happily married for over 25 years.

Over time, I had developed certain undefined feelings of guilt and remorse. When I became a Christian, I knew God had forgiven me for all of my past sin, but still these feelings lingered. As I was to discover, old feelings can be a great tool to reveal areas of unforgiveness. God showed me this through an examination of how I had dealt with my past. As a young man, I had a tendency to be somewhat self-absorbed. As a result, I didn't always care about the people I hurt. Through the years, I had learned to deal with the feelings of guilt by just casting them aside. If a memory resurfaced, I would just ignore it. Because these memories were of unresolved guilt, they kept coming back. As a result, I would occasionally fall into periods of depression or anger. As you could imagine, this could make me a very unpleasant person to be around. When I think of how my wife had to put up with my behavior during these times, it makes me feel very sorry.

What I didn't understand at the time was that even though God had forgiven me, I hadn't forgiven myself. I was instead binding myself to my own unforgiveness. There's an old expression that an idle mind is the devil's playground. This is certainly true when you have these kinds of unresolved problems. Satan will constantly keep reminding you of the things you did and also the hurt you caused. Maybe the involvement was physical as well as emotional. This can leave intense memories, adding to the difficulty of resolving the past.

In my case, I never forgave myself for the hurt I had caused others when ending some of my past relationships. This had somehow created powerful soul ties with those people. I had tried breaking them through prayer, but there was still a strong cord holding me to them. This was my cord of offense. I was bound to my own unforgiveness, and I didn't even realize it. In the grand scheme of things, this had little bearing on my life in general, but during times of great stress or fatigue, a memory would pop up. In my moments of weakness, I would begin to have all sorts of strange thoughts. From the confusion this caused, I would become unfocused or depressed. This is a dangerous place to be, because from that state all sorts of problems can occur. Fortunately, I passed through this with minimal damage. I give credit to the grace of God and a very loving wife for having kept me from going astray. Yet I wonder how many relationships have failed because of a lack of understanding and lack of self-forgiveness? While I have been fortunate, many people haven't.

When God revealed this to me, I realized that there was a root of unforgiveness that had to be removed from my life. I had a real need to forgive myself. Even though these things had happened many years ago, I now understood the need to release everything that I was holding against myself. Only then could I be truly set free. Although most of this had probably been forgotten by the people involved, (if not, please forgive me), it hadn't been forgotten by me.

As God opened my eyes, I was able to see what had happened and I asked God for forgiveness. Then I was able to forgive myself. It is almost impossible to put that moment into words. Besides a tremendous sense of peace that came over me, I felt a release in my soul that was indescribable. I had finally cut loose the ties that had bound me for all of those years. Philosopher Robert Muller put it perfectly when he said, "To forgive is the highest, most beautiful form of love. In return you will receive untold peace and happiness."

Why was this important? Because if I didn't forgive myself, how then could I truly receive God's forgiveness? I came to the realization that I had a dirty inner view of myself, even though God only saw me as clean. This had created a conflict in my soul and had opened a door for torment from the devil. Every time I hit moments of mental weakness, in would rush the enemy with accusation. It was my internal unforgiveness that fed all those feelings of guilt and remorse. By letting go, I am now free.

It is vital that you get this point. You must forgive yourself to experience complete forgiveness. This does not only apply to past relationships, but to anything that makes you feel unworthy of God's love. It is the binding and loosing principle — you must unbind yourself on earth to be unbound in heaven. For God's forgiveness to be completely realized in your life, forgive yourself.

Chapter 10

Accessing God's Forgiveness

"You can't undo anything you've already done, but you can face up to it. You can tell the truth. You can seek forgiveness, and then let God do the rest."
— **Author Unknown**

"If You, Lord, should mark iniquities, O Lord, who could stand? But there is forgiveness with You, that You may be feared." Psalm 130: 3-4

We have seen how God requires forgiveness. Now I want to look at how we can access God's forgiveness. To better understand how to seek God's forgiveness, we first must realize our need for forgiveness.

In the beginning, God created the heavens and earth. This is Genesis 1:1, the beginning of creation. When you look back on creation, you can see the beautiful plan God had for man (Adam). God had created a lush, self sustaining garden. In it was everything Adam needed, not only to survive, but to flourish and thrive. Genesis 1:29-31: *"And God said, "See, I have given you every herb that yields seed which is on the face of all the earth, and every tree whose fruit yields seed; to you it shall be for food. Also, to every beast of the earth, to every bird of the air, and to everything that creeps on the earth, in which there is life, I have given every green herb for food;" and it was so. Then God saw everything that He had made, and indeed it was very good."* God provided everything for Adam, even a mate, Eve.

God had created man for the purpose of fellowship. Besides giving him all that was needed to survive, He also created man with a free will and the ability to make choices, and God gave Adam the opportunity to make a choice.

God planted a specific tree in the garden. In Genesis 2:15-17 He gives clear instructions regarding that tree: *"Then the Lord God took the man and put him in the garden of Eden to tend and keep it. And the Lord God commanded the man, saying, "Of every tree of the garden you may freely eat, but of the tree of the knowledge of good and evil you shall not eat, for in the day that you eat of it you shall surely die."* It was simple. God had given Adam and Eve full dominion over all of the Earth. Still, He wanted to know if Adam truly trusted Him. God gave Adam and Eve a simple choice, to obey or not to obey. Eve was confronted with both temptation and a lie in chapter 3. *"Then the serpent said to the woman, "You will not surely die. For God knows that in the day you eat of it your eyes will be opened, and you will be like God, knowing good and evil." So when the woman saw that the tree was good for food, that it was pleasant to the eyes, and a tree desirable to make one wise, she took of its fruit and ate."* She made a selfish choice, but Adam, I believe, did much worse. He was created a perfect man, and I am convinced that he knew what he should have done. Unfortunately, he chose to follow Eve. *"She also gave to her husband with her, and he ate. Then the eyes of both of them were opened, and they knew that they were naked.; and they sewed fig leaves together and made themselves coverings."*

God came looking for Adam, calling for him, as He did often. Adam was now afraid, as seen in verse 10. Adam said, *"I heard Your voice in the garden, and I was afraid because I was naked; and I hid myself."* God asked Adam why he was afraid and if he had eaten from the forbidden tree. Adam's response was the first true sign of absolute selfishness. Adam blamed the woman. Eve, in turn, stated that she had been misled by the serpent.

God then cursed the serpent and told Eve that she would bear children in pain. Then to Adam He said, in verses 17-19, *"Because you have heeded the voice of your wife, and have eaten from the tree of which I commanded you, saying, 'you shall not eat of it:'" "cursed is the ground for your sake; in toil you shall eat of it all the days of your life. Both thorns and thistles it shall bring forth for you, and you shall eat the herb of the field. In the sweat of your face you shall eat bread till you return to the ground, for out of it you were taken; for dust you are, and to dust you shall return."* Adam's decision to disobey introduced sin, separation from God, and ultimately death. I think it came down to either a basic lack of trust in God or a desire to do what they believed was right for themselves. Either way, they chose to be disobedient to God. As a result, we all now bear the mark of sin.

God covered them, since they were now naked. We see this in verse 21: *"Also for Adam and his wife the LORD God made tunics of skin, and clothed them."* God made the tunics out of the skin of animals, so something had to die to cover their nakedness. This covering of nakedness is also a reference to covering their shame due to sin. By establishing the shedding of blood to cover shame and sin, God thereby established the path of redemption for man. God would now require a perfect sacrifice to bring man back to a state of full fellowship. Only a sinless man could accomplish this. Adam could have offered himself for Eve before he fell, but instead he chose to disobey. So, because God dearly loved His creation, He sent His own Son, Jesus, who was sinless, to die in the place of sinful man. Through this offering, God could forgive the debt and redeem man to Himself.

So how can we gain access to God now? Jesus said in John 3:3: *"Most assuredly, I say to you, unless one is born again, he cannot see the kingdom of God."* We must be reborn in the spirit to have restored fellowship with God. In Romans 10:9 and 10, Paul tells us how: *"that if you confess with your mouth the Lord Jesus and believe in your heart that God has raised Him from the dead, you will be saved. For with the heart one believes unto righteousness, and with the mouth confession is made unto salvation."* We must confess with our mouth and believe in our heart. By this we are saved from eternal death. It is from here that we can access all of God's forgiveness.

God wants us to come to Him willingly, and out of our desire to obey Him. Many people believe they have to be good before they can come to Jesus. This is completely wrong. You cannot ever be good enough on your own to come to Jesus. You must come as you are, now. God is present, ready to accept all who call upon Jesus' name for salvation. It is His desire and passion as seen in Romans 5:8-11: *"But God demonstrates His own love toward us, in that while we were still sinners, Christ died for us. Much more then, having now been justified by His blood, we shall be saved from wrath through Him. For if when we were enemies we were reconciled to God through the death of His Son, much more, having been reconciled, we shall be saved by His life. And not only that, but we also rejoice in God through our Lord Jesus Christ, through whom we have now received the reconciliation."* It was by the sacrifice Jesus made that we are now able to return to our designed purpose which is fellowship with God.

Forgiveness was bought and paid for at the cross. All we need to do is confess and believe. If you haven't done this in your own life, do it now. Simply ask Jesus into your life, and confess your sinful ways. Ask Him to forgive you and make you a new person on the inside. Commit to give your heart to Him and He will save you. This was the greatest decision I ever made, one that I have never regretted. As you join with Jesus, God will wash your sin clean. He will forgive all of your past and make you a new person, alive in the Spirit. A life apart from the forgiveness of God is one destined for eternal death. Accepting Jesus will bring to you the hope of eternal life.

People will ask how this God of love can send people to hell. I can tell you, He doesn't — they send themselves. The same act of selfishness that Adam showed in the garden is shown by people today who refuse to trust God. This keeps them in sin and therefore separated from God. Only through Jesus can we be reconciled to God and spare ourselves from the eternal death of hell. Only then can God's forgiveness truly be experienced. Open your heart to God, be born again, and be forgiven.

I want to leave you with a passage of scripture that I feel sums up God's complete desire to save and bring us into his forgiveness. As you read this, open up your heart to him. Seek Him and you will find that perfect peace in God's forgiveness. Titus 3:3-7: *"For we ourselves were also once foolish, disobedient, deceived, serving various lusts and pleasures, living in malice and envy, hateful and hating one another. But when the kindness and the love of God our Savior toward man appeared, not by works of righteousness which we have done, but according to His mercy He saved us, through the washing of regeneration and renewing of the Holy Spirit, whom He poured out on us abundantly through Jesus Christ our Savior, that having been justified by His grace we should become heirs according to the hope of eternal life."*

THE KEY OF FORGIVENESS-

www.ingramcontent.com/pod-product-compliance
Lightning Source LLC
Chambersburg PA
CBHW071309040426
42444CB00009B/1940